DEATH OF A MAUVE BAT

the poets experiences in and on the way to and from Toronto, Ontario, Canada by **RICK LUPERT**

DEATH OF A MAUVE BAT

Ain't Got No Press

Design, and Layout ~ Rick Lupert
Author Photo ~ Addie Lupert

Thank you Addie, Brendan, Bernie and Sara, Gerald Locklin, Sir Henry Pellatt, and all the people of Canada, especially the funny ones at Second City Toronto who made me feel famous for a few minutes.

(818) 904-1021

or

15522 Stagg Street
Van Nuys, CA 91406

or

Rick@PoetrySuperHighway.com

or

PoetrySuperHighway.com

First Edition ~ January, 2012

ISBN: 978-0-9820584-4-2 $13.00

Toronto is a kind of New York operated by the Swiss.

- Sir Peter Alexander Ustinov

Tons of movies are shot in Toronto, but Toronto is never Toronto.

- Eugene Levy

They say the camera never lies. It lies every day.

- Cesar Romero

*Skill is successfully walking a tightrope over Niagara Falls.
Intelligence is not trying.*

- anonymous

*To Addie, who undoubtedly deserves an author's credit,
and to Sir Henry Pellatt, who probably deserved better*

Everything starts with a New Jersey Wedding

They Discuss What to Do in the Event Lightning Strikes the Car

One suggests we must exit the vehicle
without touching the frame.

Another says "No, once lightning strikes,
it is done. It is only when a downed power-line
is touching the car, that you must exit carefully."

I suggest it would be better if the car is manipulated
so it doesn't come into contact with electricity.

There is much agreement.

This Could Have Been Great

There is a super funny thing I thought of
that I had forgotten by the time I remembered
to write it down. Which is now. Sorry.

It's All Me

I am excited that I have figured out
how to remotely control my computer
so I can video chat with my cats
while we're away.

I am the only one excited about this.

At The Wedding

If your love is
even a smidgen the amount
of ours

it will survive
this rain on your
outside wedding day.

Still it wouldn't hurt to
have those little umbrellas
for the cocktails.

New Grill

There is a new grill
in the Allentown backyard
you may remember last year
the previous grill was stolen.
The new grill is not secured with a chain.
This is the bold statement
of the grill buyer.

Little Help

This trip is shorter than
some of the previous ones so
I'm not sure if I'll have time to
write enough poetry to fill
an entire book.

If not, I'd appreciate it if
you could read this poem
thirty seven times.

Prophecy

In a fit of profundity I tell Addie
"the future is coming."
She agrees.

The Morning Insult

We spend the first thirty hours of our trip to Canada
in The Trivet Diner in Allentown, Pennsylvania.
This is an exaggeration, but in a place where
the coffee is merely water that has been browned
time goes at it's own pace.

Patriotism

It is the fourth of July and
I have forgotten to put on my
Red, white and blue American flag
underwear.

I will miss the planned secret sassiness
as I cross into Canada.

Perhaps I will take off my non patriotic underwear
when we get closer to the border
and give the crossing agent an extra smile.

Addie's Quote of the Day - a haiku

I'm just trying to
stay connected and I can't
even freakin' tweet.

Contingency

We stop outside
Binghamton, New York
next to a sign that says
self service dog wash.

Next time we have a dog
and are half way to Canada,
and the dog is dirty,
this is definitely
where we will come.

A Sign Westbound Through New York Says "86, Future."

Finally.

First Contact

Addie is excited by the Amish people
inside the Binghamton *Expressmart*.
In a way, I am too

Second Contact

Black Volkswagen Rabbit passes us
the driver and passenger against the headrests
in a manner too comfortable for serious driving.
They are either dead or Canadian.
It is hard to tell under these circumstances.

Halfway there

The road is long.
We have crossed the Cohocton River

half a dozen times.
Everything is green.

The roofs on the houses
The clusters of trees that know history

better than me
The fleet of John Deeres

Some say, in certain light,
even my eyes.

We are only half way but already
some license plates say Ontario.

Motley Crüe is on the radio (Dr. Feel Good)
we are saved by Zeppelin.

I see a state trooper.
It would be un-holy to be pulled over

during Led Zeppelin
a sign says *Rochester 50 miles*

I see you.
I see you.

Toronto, in which things are put in our mouths

Ethiopian Food in Toronto

It seems in every city
no matter the native ethnicity
we find ourselves at Ethiopian food.

The people at the next table talk about
the man who invented the segue.
They say he died driving his segue off a cliff.
They say it was not intentional.

This is our first night in Toronto.

Under the Influence

We watch soccer while
drinking Canadian beer in
the Irish pub on
Yonge Street.

It's pronounced *young* like
Carl, or as in not old.

It's pronounced *football*
as in the ball moves after
it comes in contact with your foot.

Clearly the tall beers are
inside us.

An Update

We are in an updated room
in our hotel.

The wallpaper that is peeling off the wall
is updated.

The door that is detached from the closet
is updated.

The elevator that we have waited
ten minutes for will soon update us
as to when it will arrive.

We will keep you
updated.

A Naked Thought

The people selling ice cream in front of
Old City Hall are all wearing dress shirts
and ties.

It seems to me if you sell ice cream
you should be naked and setting your ties
on fire.

Some of This is Fiction

In Toronto there is
Old City Hall and
New City Hall.

There is no
Middle Aged City Hall.
It's a weird Logan's Run
thing. (look it up.)

In the AGO where ekphrastia goes wild

We Should Have Looked at the Map

Because of a wrong turn we
first see only the back side of
the model boats

All the model soldiers with
their model asses pointed
at our eager faces

The Ken Thomson Collection

starts with a display case of various curios.
It's like all those little *chachkis* you
don't know what to do with that you
get as add ons to your main gift.

I tell Addie when I die,
I want her to gather up all my crap and
put it in display cases in a museum.
My enduring legacy.

The Madonna and Child With Infant St. John and Children - Andrea del Sarto

is five naked babies surrounding a woman.
Now I know what to get Addie for Christmas.

Virgin and Child - Albert Bouts

Addie describes the child as an
Old man baby

Ahh the journey begins.

Ekphrastia Gone Wild

One of the most naked statues ever
is Rodin's Adam

Oh the huge balls
the impressionist ass

At Raoul Dufy's The Yellow Violin

Addie gives a visual demonstration
of the depicted sheet music.
She becomes the painting.
She has always been the painting.

Moo-ology

Kathleen Munn's paintings include several of cows.
One is called "Study of Cows."
She never finished her cow degree though.

Touchez!

We touch the flint knapper
because the sign demands it.

My New Euphemism for Going to the Bathroom:

I had to drop Uncle Harry off at the County Fair.
Why did it take so long?
He wouldn't stop talking to his friends.

Sensitivity

Addie doesn't mean to make fun of
the culture of Inuit art, but she is concerned
that one painting could easily be referred to as
"boobs for cheeks."

Imagined instructions to accompany the sculpture "Journey to the Great Woman" by David Ruben Piqtoukun"

Take a left at the mediocre woman.

Big Woman With Little Head

is what Addie decides Henry Moore's sculpture
Draped Seated Woman should be called.

I'm keeping track of all of these so I can
write the artists and tell them what to rename their pieces.

Sole Reunion by Willie Cole
It looks like a monster made of shoes

I don't know why I bother putting
my name on these books anymore.

Addie Found Something She Can Touch in the Museum

This is going to be a while.

Canadian Fashion

They'd like you to believe that wearing
black socks with black shoes and shorts
is okay here in Canada.

They're not fooling anyone.

We get to the Canadian Art

Lots of snow.

My Zipper Has Never Worked

I find Addie alone in room of Canadian art
her hand halfway down her pants dealing with an itch.

She takes one look a me and says "oh god"
walks over and zips my fly up.

This the room of supreme confidence.

I Hope You're Reading This On the Page

I suggest the display cases would be cool
if some of them had live fish in them
not knowing I am standing in front of one
which contains a display of wooden fish.

Addie likes the idea until I tell her
it would be called an *Aquareum*.
She tells me the pun doesn't work.
I tell her it does if you spell it the way I said it.

We both laugh heartily at this
much to the chagrin of the nearby docent who
would prefer there be no noise at all.

Toronto in which the second tallest thing ever is ascended

My Compass Doesn't Point North

I am sitting across the street
from the Village Idiot Pub.

It is only by accident that I
am not inside.

The people inside wink at me.
They know what I'm about.

Verbal Phonology

A Canadian accent is not evident
on the Chinese man running the coffee shop.

Not like last night where the *aboots* came out
like it was Canada Day in their mouths.

Nordica

I think "anything goes"
is too open ended a marketing slogan
for yogurt.

Tell It Like It Is

The Toronto music garden was
designed by cellist Yo-Yo Ma,
and also, apparently, by someone with
great knowledge of landscape design
and gardening.

Free Beer

We arrive at the Steam Whistle Brewery
too late for the final tour but they
still offer the complimentary tasting so
all in all our goals have been met.

Up

If you're the kind of person
who likes to go up things and
survey the land, there's about
no more up you can go than the
CN Tower. You can see clear
to Venus from the restaurant.
You can climb to the top,
shake the hand of God.

Tired Dogs, Uninterested Cats

Addie asks what we are doing tomorrow
and then the next day.

It's not that she wants to know.
She is tired and her questions have the potential

to stall our elevation from this bench
when walking would begin.

She spots a cat in a patch of nearby trees
here under the CN tower.

It's not that she's
particularly interested in cats.

She just knows that I will go
and attempt to mingle with the cat,

further delaying the walking
to wherever it is we might be going.

The cat is not willing
to mingle.

Our feet will soon be walking
now not only with the weight

of the day upon them
but with the heaviness of

the cat who disappeared
into Canadian dusk.

Trash Night

the joy of
arriving in a new city
on trash night

the smell
the smell of welcome
the trash

the trash lining the streets
to walk beside it
on the first night

in a new city
it is
a joy

We Stop in for a Jazz Jam at the Rex on Queen Street

Any one can sign up to join in.
I can not escape the Tuesday night open mic.
A midget walks in, though in Canada he prefers to go by
Phil.

The M.C. is funny and large
She is out of breath between numbers.
She is dirty.
She is a magpie.

Three women come out of her mouth.
Two beers go in mine.
Three floors up, people do not sleep.
how could they?

A Concern

If you go to pee
unzip your fly
and can't find the hole
in your underpants
it is a problem.

The Bassist

walks
up and
down
his instrument
like it's the
freedom trail
the road
home.

Addie Photographs a Superman Curl on My Forehead

This is what I will look like tonight
when I buy a vegetarian hot dog.
They have them at stands all over the city.
Unlike in Los Angeles where if you ask
for a veggie dog at a hot dog stand,
they will laugh you into the L.A. River.

They Say it isn't Over Until the Fat Lady Sings

The lead singer of tonight's band was a fat lady.
I left the venue as soon as she took the stage.

Thinking it Through

This is the place
I want to come to when I die
or, perhaps, just before I die,
or maybe just come here and
not die at all.

Yes,
That would be best.

A Toronto Fairy Tale

Always stand in the middle
of busy intersections to
take pictures of oncoming
streetcars said the soon
to be dead woman.

Missing Sense

A blind man takes the stage
or so he thinks.

Back at The Rex

It is late but
I'm not going anywhere until
the midget takes the stage.

Apparently I Call Him Charlie

I have had almost enough alcohol
to join the band on pretty much

any song with words.
Another beer and I could

pretend to be the guitar.
A guy takes the stage

with his saxophone and
eyes like Charlie Manson

and the rest of him
a balding Chinese man.

it is his eyes we will remember
the most.

Paris Seeps In

An old French man is
taking pictures of the
whole evening.

I know he is French because
he is wearing a beret and
his hair is...
French.

You can pick up
copies of the photos
in Paris which
I plan to do.

Good Morning Toronto

This morning I almost
slit my throat shaving.
Damn this hotel.

Later at breakfast
a pineapple wedge
falls off Addie's fork
onto her plate.

That's what happened to me. I tell her.
Except it was a razor and my neck.
She laughs and tells me that's not funny
except I made it funny.

I have no choice.
This is the city of comedy
It's what I do.

Secret, Even From Me

Addie stares at a ketchup bottle
and nods knowingly. What is being
exchanged, this morning, between
the ketchup and Addie, I have no idea.

.

At the ROM where we encounter the Fanged Yogini

Real and Imagined

The Furniture of Lower Canada exhibit
is right next to the *Hall of Freaky Canadian Children.*
Only one of those is the real exhibit title.

Survival Instincts

Certain herbivorous dinosaur species
had no biological protection from predators.
They relied on behavior such as herding
to protect themselves. This is similarly how
I protect myself from obvious threats.
I surround myself with other herbivores
and begin eating the lawn.

Who Could Resist

There is frustration for everyone
when at the *Dinosaur Eggs and Babies*
exhibit, I order an omelette.

The Giant Beaver Skeleton

Oh I'm sure you can think up something
interesting to say on your own about
the giant beaver skeleton.

It's Pretty Big

We come across the ass of a rhinoceros.
It is attached to the rest of a rhinoceros
but we haven't come across that yet.

Not Going Up Or Down

I thought it was an elevator button
but it was a hole. I put my finger in a hole.
No elevator came.

Evidence I Can't Read

I misread the sign in front of the
Egyptian Tomb of Kitinis as
The Tomb of Kittens which
leads to brief disappointment
and then relief.

A Representation of the Ancient Kingdom of Egypt

There are no discernible lines
showing what would be the
current borders dividing places
like Israel and Palestine.
Maybe we should do that.
Remove the lines.

Both Addie and I Agree

The Fanged Yogini is hot.

For When I Die

We see a display of coffins from Ghana
designed to exhibit the wealth and achievements
of the deceased.

One coffin is a Mercedes Benz.
Another is a fish.

I want to be buried inside an Addie.
She is everything I have achieved.

Homesick

It is on the fourth floor
of the Royal Ontario Museum
In Toronto, Ontario, Canada
that we see large photographs
of Los Angeles Freeways.
Thousands of miles from home
we cannot escape the traffic.

Seventeen Syllables

I climb the *Stairs of
Wonder* searching for the
Urinal of Delight.

The Limits Have Been Reached

I sing my best on the spot Bing Crosbynian ballad
as we descend five levels of the *Stairs of Wonder.*
I'm covering it all, the toy soldiers, the butterflies,
the beetles, the finger bowls. A new jazz standard
is let loose into the world, improvised from my lips.
When we get to the bottom Addie tells me
We're no longer in the stairs of wonder,
so I guess you're done now
which is really more of a direction than a guess.

Artistic License

Hairless Joe
as depicted on the textile swatch

is no relation to midget Phil
from last night

or Lipless Henry
who I just made up.

Linguistic Triumph

Addie is ready for a beverage
I ask her if she wants to wait until
we get to the shoe museum where
if they have a cafe, we might be able to
get a cup of shoefee.

Not Going to Do It

There will be no poem
correlating the Bat Cave
in the Royal Ontario Museum
to Batman.

Conventional Wisdom

We pass by a chocolate cafe that offers
fondue to go. If you have chocolate fondue,
why would you need to go anywhere?

Taking a Much Needed Step Back

It takes as long as it takes
at the electric hand dryer.
So if the man in front of you
is taking a long time, it is
because his hands are not yet dry
and not because he is a whore.

At the Bata Shoe Museum where there are a lot of shoes

Parental Guidance Suggested

In the Bata Shoe Museum
or *Shoeseum* as I like to call it
we see a pair of armored tudor Sabatons
a foot (ha ha) and a half tall
the toe area shaped like a duck bill
much wider than the heel.

I'd like to see you in those Addie says.
and nothing else I respond thus once
again insuring I'll have to check the box
indicating this book contains material
which may not be appropriate for children
on the publication forms.

Shoebservation

It seems to me
there are a lot of shoes
in display cases here.
It reminds me a lot

of being in a shoe store.
Except for the display cases

and the occasional appearance
of moccasins.

I'm Looking at Shoes

You could put anything
in display cases and
call it a museum.
I've got a few extra forks.
Throw in an informative video
and it's time to apply for
non-profit status.

I Imagined I Was Being Hilarious

For a while I stood
at the entrance of the
shoe museum staring at
the shoes of incoming visitors
and shaking my head
discouragingly.

This Museum Lasts Until The End of the Sky

Finally we get to the fourth level
which is shoes in art. It is all
paintings of shoes, or at least
paintings of people wearing shoes.

It is all still life.

There Is No Typo In This Poem

At the end
we go to the
gift shoep.

Puns Exchanged at the Gift Shoep

R: Do you get a lot of people referring to this as the gift shoep?

S: No but a lot of people say this place has a lot of sole.

R: That's a pedestrian effort.

S: That's a good one.

Casa Loma
where secrets
are easily
discovered

Display of Wealth

Sir Henry Pellatt's celery vase
was a custom made gift.
Its purpose was to display
celery, a rarity in Toronto.

These days in America
celery hides in chopped salad
disguised as lost children
longing to peanut butter.

Sleuthing

Sir Henry had a secret staircase from
his study down to the wine cellar.
We know this because of the large sign
that says secret staircase with an
arrow pointing to the secret staircase.

Permanent Recession

In 1938, fourteen years after he
was forced to sell and leave the castle he built,
Henry Pellatt returned to Casa Loma.

He walked the halls as an honored guest
of the Kiwanis club of West Toronto.
He saw his bedroom and study

the unfinished swimming pool.
He had built this place
but was no longer home.

Badum Bum

Casa Loma was the first home in Toronto
with running water. The water is still running.
They have been chasing it for ninety years.

More Sleuthing

On the east side of Casa Loma
there is a secret garden. We know this
because of the sign that says Secret Garden.
If you've read this poem. It is already too late.
Dead men tell no tales.

Ode to H.G. Wells

We see a blind man's cane
on a picnic table outside
Casa Loma. There is no blind man.
It's possible he is invisible.

Audibility

We are walking by
the Canadian Hearing Society

I purposefully mumble to Addie.
What? she says

and I repeat what I had just said
my plan working perfectly.

COURAGE MY LOVE   14

Toronto where I
am given a free
blue drink for
going with it

The Unknown Shower

Oh hotel shower.
The way you turn from
hot to cold with no
effort from me.
Oh the unknown.
It is hot.
It is cold.
It is hot again.
Oh cold.
Not a flick of
my wrist on
a knob.
It just happens.
It is magic.
The city of magic.
Doug Henning lived
here, and died here.
Oh hotel shower.
Should I put on
a sweater, or
sunscreen. Time
for breakfast. A
magic breakfast.
My eggs will speak
of you. The Niagara
of Bloor Street.

Starstruck

We go to place advertising
famous all day breakfasts.
I ask for the autograph
of an omelette at midnight.

Rules of Engagement

An announcement in the subway station
says, when the train arrives, we should not
charge the doors. As a result I have
cancelled the gathering of my army.
I will simply walk on the train and
then civilly dismember everyone with
my sword of humility.

footnote:
When we arrive at the Spadina station
a woman is clearly charging the entrance
making it difficult for us to exit.
She is the problem.

In the Absence of a Wishbone

Addie and I grasp both ends
of a french fry at the Mill Street
Brew pub and pull it in half.
I don't think either of us made wishes
so perhaps it wasn't in the absence of
a wishbone, but rather it was just
our time to join forces and
rip a french fry in half.

The Old Neighborhood

What happened to all the Jews
in all these neighborhoods in
all these cities that used to be
all Jewish?

We have moved away.
We are not as many as we were.
We live in Van Nuys
We are just
holding on.

Not Even Going To Ask

According to a poster
The Bedlam All Girl
Pillow Fight Review
is happening tonight.
I suspect we won't
be making it to that.

The Kensington Market Area is Populated Completely by Mexicans and Lesbians *

This exhaustive demographic
study was conducted by
walking quickly down one street
and then taking a left.

* and two guys from Portugal selling Cheese.

The New Old Neighborhood

The Augusta Street neighborhood
near Kensington is like Melrose was
before Gucci moved in. When you
could be invited to *Nam Myoho Renge Kyo*
and buy incense on every corner.
Wacko. Soap Plant. La Luz de Jesus.
You know what I'm talking about.

Shut The Fuck Up

The video film *Shut The Fuck Up*
by the Toronto collective General Idea
documents their performance painting
exhibition in Geneva, 1983, called *XXX Blue*
which included three stuffed poodles,
made by taxidermists, used as brushes
to paint giant blue X's onto canvases
and also footage of the seventies Joker
winning an art contest for his blank
painting *Death of a Mauve Bat.*

This is still not a poem about Batman
after seeing The Bat Cave at the ROM.

More Evidence of My Illiteracy

I misread a sign on Queen street
as *Buttock Pants* when it really says
Button Pants. I guess both make sense.
But only one is delightfully hysterical.

Boom

I pick up a copy of
Spontaneous Combustion Magazine
before it's too late.

A Pattern Develops

We pass by a sign that I think says
The Healthy Buttock which really says
The Healthy Butcher.

Buttock is funny.

The Cheese King

We are impressed by the architecture
of the cheese at *La Fenice* on King Street.
The waiter tells us it is the King of Parmesan Cheese.

I ask if I should bow but
there is no time for my tomfoolery.
He tells us the story of the cheese.

In Italy as the second world war came
They would bury the cheese with
proper moisture to protect it from...

well he didn't say if they were protecting
it from the Nazis or the Allies.
I guess anyone would have wanted this cheese.

So they buried it as peasant cheese and then,
when the war was over, they dug it up and
it became King. This is the story of the cheese.

At another table they talk about how
Nancy Reagan has reunited with Ronny.
Across the street, something about Fellini.

I bow anyway. It's the least
I could do for the cheese...
and the people who made it.

Waiting For Liz

The next table decides to wait for Liz
before ordering their drinks. God forbid
they should be drunk before Liz arrives.
From what I know of Liz it's a good call.

The Royal Affair Continues

Addie announces the arrival of the pasta spoons. Again, I am not sure if I should bow.

Second City

The ongoing study of comedy continues as
we decide to take in a show at Second City
a stalwart of modern comedy in the world.

*I like the way people choose words and speak
them out loud in a certain order.*

In the line outside the venue everyone
is very serious. We are saving our laughter
for inside. We distract ourselves with talk of
death so the words inside will work as they should.

*The walls lined with photos of those
who came before...some of whom are dead.*

This isn't funny.

Now, Now, No

All week we've been looking for *Now*
the entertainment guide to Toronto
to help us figure out what to do at night.
We finally see the new issue Thursday,
when we already have plans, causing me
to say *Now 'Now?' No!*

Discovered

They brought me on stage
at *Second City Toronto.*
I breathed in a funny manner
and answered their improvised
questions to the delight of the audience.
I received a free blue drink for my effort.
My feet stood where others have stood.
I would stand there again.

Foodaism

Montreal had it's poutine and
for us, Toronto was about the
veggie dogs on every street corner.
We ate one in Dundas Square
before heading back to the hotel.
It made the night last longer.

Don't Stay Or Eat Here

All I can say
about the continental breakfast
at the *Town Inn Suites* is
that it was indeed served
on a continent.

Niagara Falls, where disposable ponchos destroy the world

A World Wonder

So this is it
a world wonder
Niagara Falls.

We don disposable blue ponchos
and ride an elevator to a boat
which takes us into the mist.

Across the river
America, land of the me,
home of the...

Signals are bouncing.
our cell phones can't decide
what country they are in.

The world dies a little
as we put on our second
disposable poncho of the day.

We are preparing to go
Behind the Falls. I am
reminded of the joke

on the *Jungle Cruise* where
They take you behind the Falls
and call it the back side of water.

Addie says
she is thirsty.
I point.

Even the Amish are here
Behind the Falls. Everyone
wants to see God's wonders.

We are an army dressed in
yellow plastic. The enemy is the wet.
The poncho, our defense.

More gallons of water pass
in front of us than we can count.
We could power Toronto,

build a Casa Loma
get in a barrel and pray.
We wouldn't want to count.

At the end you can buy
anything with the words
Niagara Falls on it

a shot glass
a thimble
a picture of you.

In the right restaurant here
they'll carve your image into a steak.
They'll make a gravy falls,

a mashed potato Mist Maid.
I keep forgetting I'm not in America.
I wish everyone would forget.

This Happened

A man buys a coke
from a machine with a picture
of the Falls on it.

I wonder what he think about
as the drink falls down his throat

Reflecting on Toronto

In order to get through
one of the daily itineraries
you need the endurance of a Cylon
Addie says.

I stopped her right there on Yonge Street
held her tightly. Told her I love her.

Later on I referred to the Skylon tower
in Niagara falls as the Cylon tower.

She knew what I meant
which made me love her
all the more.

Belated Patriotism

We missed fireworks on the fourth of July
so watching them on the eighth in Canada
shot over the American Niagara Falls
seems like the best idea we've ever had.
The fireworks sail out on a boat.
Addie is in the bathroom somewhere in Canada.
I hope she comes back before the famous boom.

Shoes May Or May Not Be Required

We pass by the Shoeless Joe restaurant
which doesn't seem like the kind of place
you could walk into barefoot. We think it
would be funny if there was a sign in the
front that said "No shirt, no shoes, No service."
There is no such sign and as a result
we have nothing to report here.

At the Hilton

I want to live in our room at
The Niagara Falls Hilton for
the rest of my life.

On the other hand
after our room in Toronto
you could tar and feather me

and I would assume it's room
service.

Dreams Deferred

We ask the waitress at breakfast
if she wouldn't mind taking our picture
with the Falls in the background.

(They don't say "Niagara" here
like in China where they just
call it "food.")

She is happy to oblige and
a photo shoot ensues as she
takes us through her daily
routine of poses in her favorite spots.

She says she wants to be a
photographer in her next life.
I wonder why she doesn't start
in this one.

No day but today.

Sentience

The robot elevators
move up and down the Skylon tower
probably planning the annihilation
of the human race, but for now,
just moving people to the observation tower.

Luperts In The Mist

They say Niagara Falls is the
honeymoon capital of the world.

*No, my love, it is anywhere I go
with you.*

Oh

Canada.

Epilogue in which the fate of the characters is revealed

Epilogue in which the fate of the characters is revealed

Am I Really Ending This Book with a Bathroom Poem?

Airplane bathrooms don't have windows
which is fine. The view would be nice
but this way high altitude birds and
looky-loo astronauts can't see you
doing your business.

The Author in a well-planned photo at the Royal Ontario Museum

About The Author

Rick Lupert has been involved in the Los Angeles poetry community since 1990. He served for two years as a co-director of the Valley Contemporary Poets, a non-profit organization which produces readings and publications out of the San Fernando Valley. His poetry has appeared in numerous magazines and literary journals, including *The Los Angeles Times, Rattle, Chiron Review, Zuzu's Petals, Caffeine Magazine, Blue Satellite* and others. He edited the anthologies *A Poet's Haggadah: Passover through the Eyes of Poets*, and *The Night Goes on All Night - Noir Inspired Poetry*, and is the author of thirteen other books: *Sinzibuckwud!, We Put Things In Our Mouths, Paris: It's The Cheese, I Am My Own Orange County, Mowing Fargo, I'm a Jew. Are You?, Feeding Holy Cats, Stolen Mummies, I'd Like to Bake Your Goods, A Man With No Teeth Serves Us Breakfast* (Ain't Got No Press), *Lizard King of the Laundromat, Brendan Constantine is My Kind of Town* (Inevitable Press) and *Up Liberty's Skirt* (Cassowary Press). He has hosted the long running Cobalt Café reading series in Canoga Park since 1994 and is regularly featured at venues throughout Southern California.

Rick created and maintains the Poetry Super Highway, a major internet resource for poets. (PoetrySuperHighway.com)

Currently Rick works as a music teacher at synagogues in Southern California and as a graphic and web designer for anyone who would like to help pay his mortgage.

Rick's Other Books

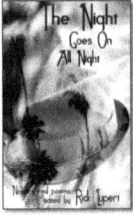

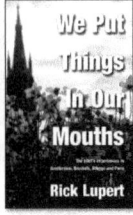

The Night Goes On All Night
Noir Inspired Poetry (edited by)
Ain't Got No Press ~ November, 2011

Sinzibuckwud!
Ain't Got No Press ~ January, 2011

We Put Things In Our Mouths
Ain't Got No Press ~ January, 2010

A Poet's Haggadah (edited by)
Ain't Got No Press ~ April, 2008

A Man With No Teeth
Serves Us Breakfast
Ain't Got No Press ~ May, 2007

I'd Like to Bake Your Goods
Ain't Got No Press ~ January, 2006

Stolen Mummies
Ain't Got No Press ~ February, 2003

Brendan Constantine is My Kind of Town
Inevitable Press ~ September, 2001

Up Liberty's Skirt
Cassowary Press ~ March, 2001

Feeding Holy Cats
Cassowary Press ~ May, 2000

I'm a Jew, Are You?
Cassowary Press ~ May, 2000

Mowing Fargo
Sacred Beverage Press ~ December, 1998

Lizard King of the Laundromat
The Inevitable Press ~ February, 1998

I Am My Own Orange County
Ain't Got No Press ~ May, 1997

Paris: It's The Cheese
Ain't Got No Press ~ May, 1996

For more information:
http://PoetrySuperHighway.com/

www.ingramcontent.com/pod-product-compliance
Lightning Source LLC
LaVergne TN
LVHW051102080426
835508LV00019B/2021

9780982058442